This Book Belongs To:

MW00452448

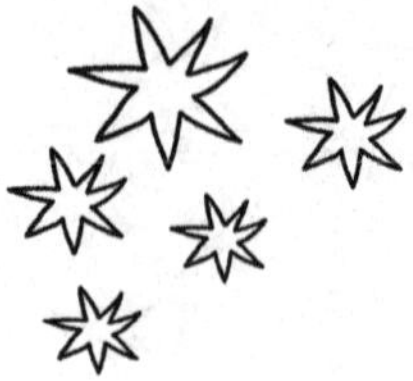

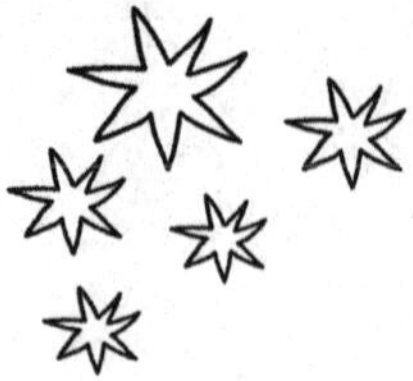

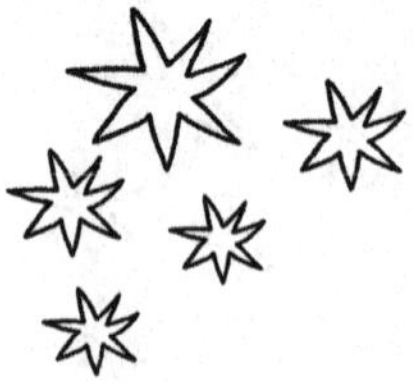

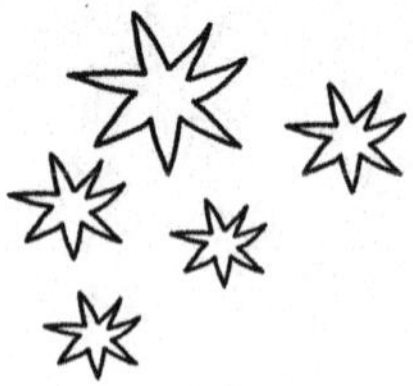

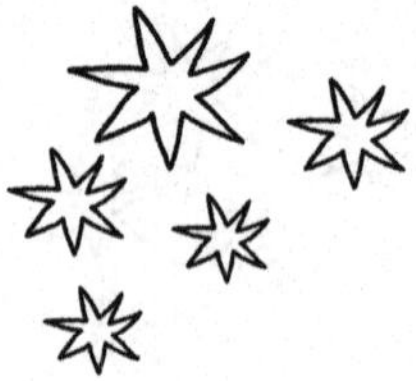

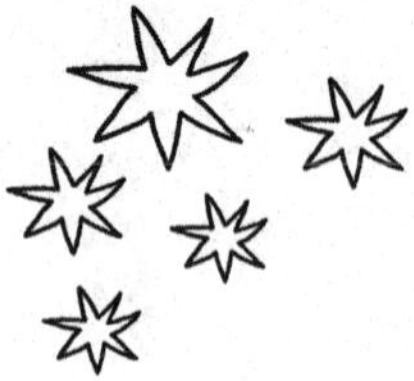

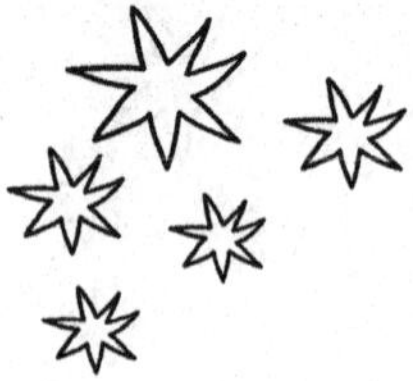

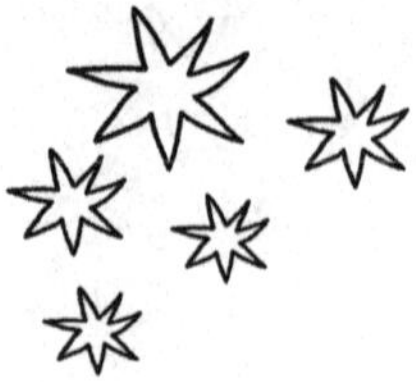

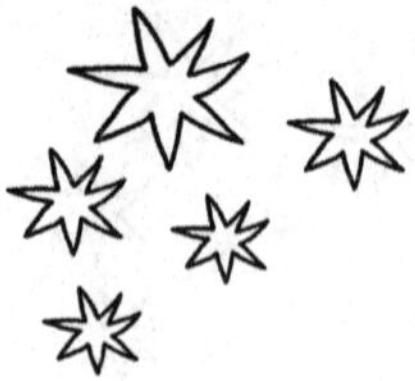

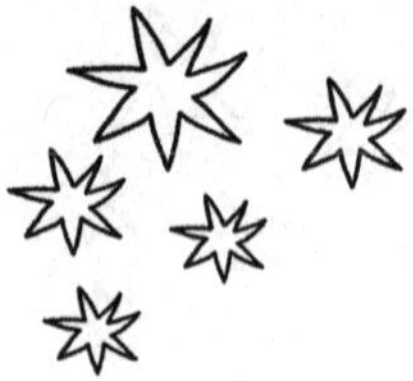

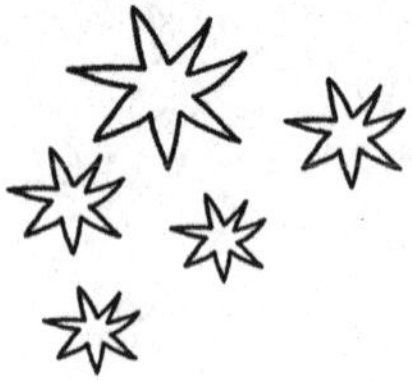

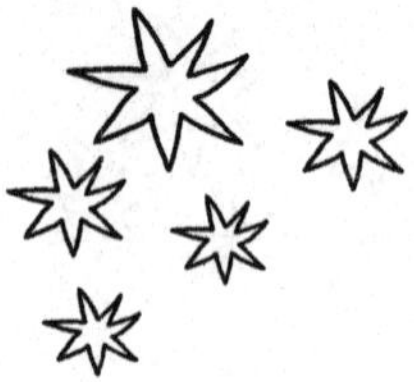

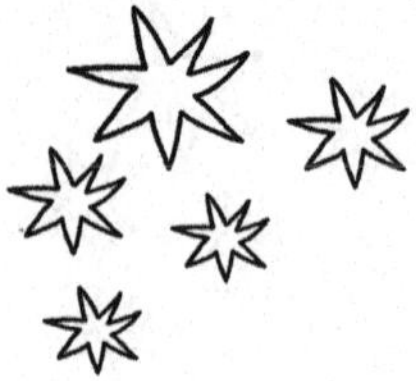

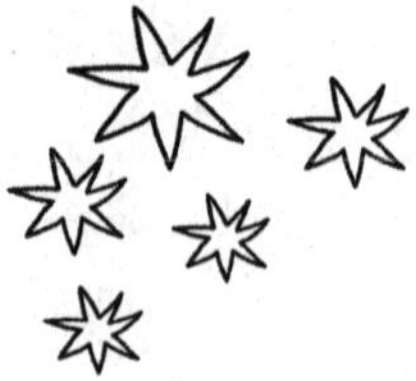

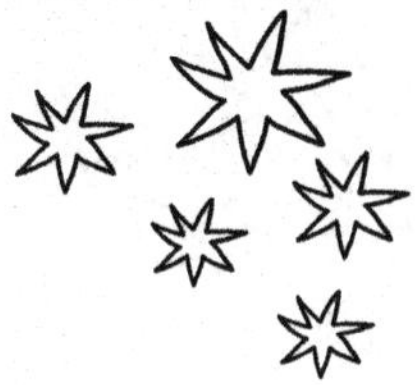